More Glimpses of Communion

Presiding Over Communion
For the Lord's Church

A Reference Handbook

For Communion Speakers

Grady W. Troute

To the Women of My Family

Sharon Lee Shipley Troute

My Wife, My Love, My Inspiration

Charlotte Adele Legate Troute

My First Wife Who is With Her Savior,

The Mother of My Children

Rebecca Lynn Troute Crook

My Daughter, a Fine Mother, and a Delightful Joy

My Granddaughters

Sierra Charlotte Crook, and Cheyenne Reta Crook

Who Make My Heart Happy

TABLE OF CONTENTS

FOREWORD BY WADE MCKNIGHT

In my time under the eldership of Grady, in Centerville OH, I grew to love his heart and admire his knowledge of the scriptures. Many times we had the discussion of how important it was to keep the Communion service from becoming rote and to keep the depth of the LORD's sacrifice at the front of our minds. That is why I was so pleased to hear Grady planned to share this passion in written form. In his first book, "Glimpses of Communion," Grady Troute gave us a year's worth of devotionals for the Communion service for the Lord's Church. As I read through another year's worth in, "More Glimpses," I was once again struck by the conclusion of how there is a thread throughout the entire Bible that leads us to our Savior, Jesus Christ. Time and again as Grady shares scriptures from the Old and New Testaments, what we discover is Jesus and his sacrifice for us. In short devotionals, that anyone can share, we are reminded of why we unify each week to remember this sacrifice and how important it is that we focus solely on this as we partake of the body and the blood.

Wade McKnight

Family Minister, Southern Oaks Church of Christ

Chickasha, OK

INTRODUCTION

This book was written for those who preside over the communion table. God bless every man who does so. If this is a path you have chosen, then your job is both noble and difficult. That Christ died for mankind is at the very center of Christian thought. It would be ideal if the heart of every member of the congregation could be taken into the shadow of the cross to think the profound thoughts of the crucifixion. This ideal case is quite unlikely for almost all congregations, because members are at differing levels of maturity in their Christian walk. The communion comments alone can help, but the growth of understanding requires continued pursuit of the deeper matters of mankind's relationship with the Savior.

The hope of this author is that this book of communion themes and its predecessor will make at least a meaningful difference in that:

- Communion will move closer to being a centerpiece of the Sunday worship,
- Participation will become a longed for, rich and rewarding experience for members to anticipate,
- Hearts will be touched in ways that encourage a closer walk with the Savior, and
- Communion will not be thought of simply as a chore to be completed.

What the Book Is

This book contains 52 communion themes, enough for one year of communions. Together with my previous book on the same subject, there are 104 themes, enough for two years. The themes can be used directly without modification, but this may not be the best use. The author believes that a communion speaker is benefited the most by using the themes in the book as thought starters. The ideas in the themes can then be modified to fit the given congregation and the speaker's delivery style. Also, thoughts from multiple themes can be combined in various ways. This course of action will develop the speaker's ability to compose his own themes.

What the Book is Not

The book is not presented as a correction of all problems associated with communion. It is presented as an aid. It does come with the prayers of the author that your communions will become richer and more meaningful. With some congregations, communion is displaced far from its intended central role. Much love and teaching will be required to bring it to its New Covenant appointed place.

What the Book Can Be

Communion comments are essentially short devotionals focusing upon the crucifixion and the meaning of the bread and the fruit of the vine. Many devotionals involve redemption by the blood of our Savior. Hence, many of the themes, with minor modifications, can be made into devotional messages. It is also true that many communion speakers also serve to deliver devotional addresses. Hence, the book and its predecessor can be useful in both needs.

May Thoughts of Communion Bring You

Dedication, Peace, and Gratitude

THEME 1: REMINDERS
COMMUNION COMMENTS

It is time to pay tribute to our Savior by remembering the crucifixion. These emblems before us, the bread and the fruit of the vine, represent respectively the body and the blood of our Lord. The thoughts that come immediately to mind are:

- Christ's great sacrifice, and
- How great the love of God for mankind must be.

Communion may not be conducted any way we choose. Paul discusses this in I Corinthians 11:17-34:

- The form must be appropriate. It is to be focused and orderly.
- The substance must recognize the true meaning of the emblems, the bread and the fruit of the vine.

The communion and the emblems are reminders to help us remember who we are and the path God wants us to walk. We are a human organization with all the frailties of human nature. We need the reminders to keep us on course.

We commune as one. That has vast implications:

- Our hearts and minds are joined.
- There are no social castes. We are all unworthy servants redeemed by Christ's sacrifice.
- We each want all to be saved, and
- Our joined hearts provide the temple where God dwells in the Spirit.

What do we have as God's gift to us?

- We have an eternal King, Jesus Christ.
- We have a path to walk, specified by the New Covenant.
- We have a destiny, to live with God for eternity.

Prayer for the Bread – The Emblem is Served

Prayer for the Wine–The Emblem is Served

THEME 2: ALONE
COMMUNION COMMENTS

It is time for Christians at this location to commune with our Lord. These emblems, the bread and the wine, represent respectively the body and blood of our Savior. It is a time of great respect and humility. We are asked to remember the day He died for us.

Most of us have had a time in life when things were going badly, and we felt very alone. We may have had friends, but it seemed they were of little consolation. The pain and unhappiness were uniquely ours, and the world went on, seemingly indifferent. The depth of our feelings may have prevented us from recognizing the efforts of true friends.

Job was a prominent wealthy father. He lost his children, his wealth, and his health. His body was covered with sores, and he was completely miserable. Oh, he had friends, and they were true friends. But they thought he was responsible for his situation due to some failure before God. In the depths of his sorrow, he made these declarations:

Job 16:19-20
[19] Even now my witness is in heaven; my advocate is on high.
[20] My intercessor is my friend as my eyes pour out tears to God;

Job 19:25-26

[25] I know that my Redeemer lives, and that in the end he will stand upon the earth. [26] And after my skin has been destroyed, yet in my flesh I will see God;

Job did not accept that he was alone. Irrespective of how he received this special knowledge from God, he held fast to it and retained his faith and hope. Job's faith that a Redeemer lives and will ultimately stand on the earth was a shadow to Job that became reality when Christ walked the earth. This shadow to Job is clear to us. Christ is a beacon that can shine through any storm of life.

In these emblems is the promise that we will never be left alone. We have a Redeemer and Witness who pleads for us. He joins us in this communion.

Prayer for the Bread – The Emblem is Served

Prayer for the Wine–The Emblem is Served

THEME 3:
THE BATTLE IS THE LORD'S
COMMUNION COMMENTS

COMMENTS BEFORE THE BREAD

It is time for Christians at this location to commune with
our Lord. These emblems, the bread and the wine, represent
respectively the body and blood of our Savior. It is a time of
great respect and humility. We are asked to remember the
day He died for us.

The Bible records many great moments. One such moment
is a favorite with young people and adults alike. A young
shepherd boy, David, confronted a giant, seasoned warrior,
Goliath. Goliath was backed up by a confident Philistine
army. David was backed up by an army where most were
afraid to be where he stood. Goliath threatened and insulted
David. David's response included these words:

> **1 Samuel 17:47**
> *⁴⁷ All those gathered here will know that it is
> not by sword or spear that the Lord saves;
> for the battle is the Lord's ...*

We who gather about this table as God's royal priesthood
may be encircled by forces vast and intimidating as we live

our lives. We are precious to God. He has made us a royal priesthood. He gave His son for us. We can stand our ground and be assured that the battle will be won.

Prayer for the Bread – The Emblem is Served

COMMENTS BEFORE THE WINE

Who is this awesome God who stands behind us and does not lose? In this moment while we remember His gift to us, it will frame our thoughts if we consider His Great Champion Who communes with us today:

> ### Revelation 5:11-12
> *[11] Then I looked and heard the voice of many angels, numbering thousands upon thousands, and ten thousand times ten thousand. They encircled the throne and the living creatures and the elders.*
> *[12] In a loud voice they sang: "Worthy is the Lamb, who was slain, to receive power and wealth and wisdom and strength and honor and glory and praise!"*

Prayer for the Wine–The Emblem is Served

THEME 4:
SOMETHING PRECIOUS
COMMUNION COMMENTS

COMMENTS BEFORE THE BREAD

King Josiah (II Kings 22 & 23)

Josiah became king at the tender age of eight. The nation was adrift, but Josiah reached out to God nevertheless. In his 18th year something wonderful happened during renovations to the temple. The book of the law was found. The people of God had drifted so far that they had even lost the law that God gave Moses. Josiah was very distraught, even ripped his garments, when the law was read to him. He immediately recognized just how much they were displeasing God. Josiah then dedicated himself to a return to the paths of God. He purged the land of unholy priests and practices. He cleared away signs, symbols, and people dedicated to false Gods. He commanded that the Passover celebration be resumed. And so it was.

Josiah's case is not a direct parallel with communions practiced in our congregations today. Indeed, in virtually every congregation we have, the bread and the fruit of the vine have not been lost nor forgotten. However, the communion is so precious that there is a need to move it more to the center of life and worship. That is, to make pervasive in our hearts the stark reality that Deity walked this earth and died for each of us.

Prayer for the Bread – The Emblem is Served

COMMENTS BEFORE THE WINE

Christ's Sacrifice–The Centerpiece

Consider an elegant dinner designed to honor a very important guest. The table is spread with the finest dinnerware in the house. The house is spotless. All things have been made ready, except one. The centerpiece on the table is a wilted and browning bouquet of flowers. Petals and leaves have fallen on the table. The vase is dirty, and the water has a stench. Is this similar to a church service that sparkles well in terms of songs, sermon, and prayers, and yet … no true effort of heart is paid to the centerpiece, the communion? What if communion becomes a ritual just to get done? I would contend that, in this case, something precious has been lost.

The Lord's Supper – A Continual Memorial

Our communion is a continual memorial in the same sense as the Passover. The Passover feast is a shadow; the communion is the reality. Christ is the sacrificial lamb.

Unlike the temple of Josiah's time, the temple of the New Covenant is not a physical place. It is an edifice of living stones, members making up the church. If we lose the precious value of communion in our hearts, we may yet find it

24

when we perform the scripturally required self examination. Renovations may be necessary to take these emblems in a way that honors our Savior.

Prayer for the Wine–The Emblem is Served

THEME 5: CONTINUANCE
COMMUNION COMMENTS

It is time for Christians at this location to commune with our Lord. These emblems, the bread and the wine, represent respectively the body and blood of our Savior. It is a time of great respect and humility. We are directed to look deeply into our hearts and discern the body and blood of Christ on the cross. We are asked to remember the day He died for us.

We often yearn for peace in our lives. The pace and problems of this world cause us to want something stable and soothing. The oceans can be soothing. We seem to be attuned to the rhythmic waves of the ocean. Cultures of man come and go on its shores. The enterprises of man along its shores vanish, but the ocean continues to lap away the years. We can be lulled into thinking that it will go on forever. But it won't. It is a created thing.

The day will come when God decides to pull the curtain on created things. We are told in Hebrews 12 that God will shake the heavens and the earth. We are told that there is one thing that cannot be shaken. It is the church, and we are in it. We do have an anchor, but it is not for the ocean. It reaches through the veil to God. When created things are shaken, we will be protected by His promises. Christ made this possible by His death on the cross.

Prayer for the Bread – The Emblem is Served

Prayer for the Wine–The Emblem is Served

THEME 6: CHOICES
COMMUNION COMMENTS

It is time for Christians at this location to commune with our Lord. These emblems, the bread and the wine, represent respectively the body and blood of our Savior. It is a time of great respect and humility. We are asked to remember the day He died for us.

Joshua confronted the Israelites with a dramatic choice:

> **Joshua 24:15**
> *[15] But if serving the Lord seems undesirable to you, then choose for yourselves this day whom you will serve, whether the gods your forefathers served beyond the River, or the gods of the Amorites, in whose land you are living. But as for me and my household, we will serve the Lord."*

When we reflect on our lives, it seems that an accurate summary can be made from simply a list of the important choices. Most of us can remember the more important decisions we have made. Some decisions have consequences with long lives. Some are good; others are regretted.

The communion gives us a weekly confrontation with ourselves. We are asked to examine our hearts to see if the choice we made to follow Christ is still being honored. We are asked to discern the body and blood of our Lord. It is as if He is asking us, "Do you remember what I did for you?"

Prayer for the Bread – The Emblem is Served

Prayer for the Wine–The Emblem is Served

THEME 7: UNTHINKABLE
COMMUNION COMMENTS

It is time for Christians at this location to commune with our Lord. These emblems, the bread and the wine, represent respectively the body and blood of our Savior. It is a time of great respect and humility. We are asked to remember the day He died for us.

God picked Abraham to be the father of a multitude of nations. Abraham and Sarah were old, well stricken with age, when God gave to them the son of promise, Isaac. God had promised Abraham that through his seed, all nations would be blessed.

Then God asked of Abraham the unthinkable!

> **Genesis 22:2**
> [2] *Then God said, "Take your son, your only son, Isaac, whom you love, and go to the region of Moriah. Sacrifice him there as a burnt offering on one of the mountains I will tell you about."*

It is difficult for us to conceive of such a thing. Abraham had great faith and moved to obey God, but we can be confident that it wrenched his heart and brought horror to his mind. He would have complied with God's command had God's angel not stayed his hand. Abraham passed the test of his willingness to obey.

Among the many profound questions of the scriptures is this one, "Why did God ask of Abraham the exact thing that He would later do for the heirs of Abraham, namely, sacrifice His Son?" Who are the heirs of Abraham?

Galatians 3:26-29
²⁶ You are all sons of God through faith in Christ Jesus,
²⁷ for all of you who were baptized into Christ have clothed yourselves with Christ.
²⁸ There is neither Jew nor Greek, slave nor free, male nor female, for you are all one in Christ Jesus.
²⁹ If you belong to Christ, then you are Abraham's seed, and heirs according to the promise.

We are! Of all races of mankind! Of all social levels! Male and female! All who have "put on" Christ in baptism have been granted the right to gather around this table as heirs of Abraham. What God asked of Abraham, He did for us.

He did the unthinkable! He sacrificed His Son!

Prayer for the Bread – The Emblem is Served

Prayer for the Wine–The Emblem is Served

31

THEME 8: ALL POWER
COMMUNION COMMENTS

Christ made a declaration to His disciples after His crucifixion and before His ascension. It was staggering in its enormity:

> **Matthew 28:18**
> *[18] Then Jesus came to them and said, "All authority in heaven and on earth has been given to me ..."*

During communion we remember Him on the cross, abused, alone, and in agony. That's not how He is now. His work was finished on the cross. Satan was delivered a mighty blow. Satan's power of death over us was taken from him. Those of the church have been ransomed by the death of our Savior.

John's vision of Christ in Revelation 1 is that of One standing among seven candlesticks representing the seven churches of Asia. His appearance is awesome. The churches, as candlesticks, are to provide light. This is a duty we have, and it is directly related to how much we love the Savior and honor His directions. We are reminded of His authority by His chilling warning to the church at Ephesus.

> **Revelation 2:5**
> *[5] Remember the height from which you have fallen! Repent and do the things you did at*

> *first. If you do not repent, I will come to you*
> *and remove your lampstand from its place.*

They had left their first love. The mighty Savior can move their candlestick from its place. It is Christ who reigned over the church at Ephesus, and He reigns here.

While we commune, we must discern His body and blood as we take these emblems. We need to remember with humility the first love that brought us to Christ.

Prayer for the Bread – The Emblem is Served

Prayer for the Wine–The Emblem is Served

THEME 9: SHARING
COMMUNION COMMENTS

Most of us have experienced life situations that troubled and tested us. It is common to expect compassion from those closest to us. Christ was deeply troubled when He came to Gethsemane. A severe ordeal was eminent. He asked His disciples to wait and watch while He prayed. While He agonized and prayed, they went to sleep. In these few minutes, we will commune and recall Gethsemane. He wants us to be fully awake and aware.

When He was betrayed and arrested, He had the choice to ask His Father for twelve legions of angels to save Him. He chose instead to follow His path to death for us. He wants us to consider now the gravity of that decision with respect to mankind.

The High priest and the ruling council spat upon Him and struck Him. He wants us think on these things during this communion.

With Pontius Pilate, He was whipped, humiliated, forced to wear a crown of thorns, and sentenced to be crucified. He wants us to remember these things; He wants us to realize that we must be ready to accept the same fate as He if it awaits us.

Christ walked a path from Pilate to Golgotha because of love, duty, and compassion. He wants us to walk with Him in our minds now and be willing to walk with Him in life even to death for our Christianity.

Now, as we take these emblems, we are to discern the body and blood of God's Son, as He died for us.

Prayer for the Bread – The Emblem is Served

Prayer for the Wine–The Emblem is Served

THEME 10: STING
COMMUNION COMMENTS

Most of us can remember a time when we did something selfish, something that helped us and hurt others. Some are quite content with such actions. Others, with a more healthy conscience, remember with regret.

Likewise, most of us can remember a time when we did something sacrificial for someone because we felt it was the right thing to do. Most people who do something sacrificial remain happy with their decision, but not always. Some have come to use the expression,

"No good deed ever goes unpunished".

There is bitterness in that expression. Is it the expression of persons who have been hurt for doing something good and noble? Good deeds sometimes have a cost in pain and/ or sacrifice. Is that a proof that we should just be selfish to avoid the hurt?

Sometimes, but not always, age brings a maturity that answers the question:

- The benefits gained by selfish deeds fade and leave only a bitter memory from a time when we were less mature.
- The hurts that came from doing something good usually heal and we are left with the sweet knowledge that we did something good and noble.

· A good rule becomes, "Do sacrificial things that help others. The memory is much better."

There is an old story about a father who did something sacrificial for his child. I am not aware of the origin, but I feel quite sure that such a sacrifice has been made by both fathers and mothers when the situation demanded. The story unfolds as follows:

A wasp landed on a baby and was walking on the child. The father scooped up the wasp in his hand and crushed it. A bystander commented, "I'm surprised that it didn't sting you". The father replied, "It did".

We are created in God's image. Life goes better when we display His image within us. He took a terrible sting for us when His Son died on the cross. He gave us an answer as to how to live:

Live a life of sacrifice to others.

The outcome far exceeds any momentary consequences.

These emblems, the bread and the fruit of the vine, represent respectively the body and blood of our Savior. It is a time of great respect and humility. We are directed to look deeply into our hearts and discern the body and blood of Christ on the cross. We are asked to remember the day when our Savior died for us, the day when God's love freed us from the sting of death.

Prayer for the Bread – The Emblem is Served

Prayer for the Wine–The Emblem is Served

THEME 11:
THE LOWLY BIRTH
COMMUNION COMMENTS

It is time for us to commune with our Lord. We are called to think about the day when our Savior died for our sins. These emblems before us represent His body and blood. Each has profound spiritual meanings.

Most believers are touched in their hearts when they consider the day Christ was crucified. There is perhaps as much or more emphasis placed upon our Savior's birth. Our children can tell us about:

- The star in the East,
- The wise men who saw it,
- The three gifts they brought, and
- The shepherds who experienced a multitude of angels praising God.

One image that seems always present is that the birth occurred in a manger, quite a lowly birth for God's Son. That aspect has been the subject of many discussions and sermons. Just like the widow's mite; however, importance cannot be judged by earthly appearances.

This important observation should be made. There is little distance in God's view between a person born of low estate and a person born in a royal bed. That is only a small step. Christ made a step of vast distance when He left equality with God to become human, even a servant.

We are to be of the same mind as Christ as we live life and especially as we partake of these emblems. Putting aside pretenses of self importance, we partake as servants thankful to our Lord.

Prayer for the Bread – The Emblem is Served

Prayer for the Wine–The Emblem is Served

THEME 12: UNCALLED
COMMUNION COMMENTS

It is time for Christians at this location to commune with our Lord. These emblems, the bread and the wine, represent respectively the body and blood of our Savior. It is a time of great respect and humility.

Great events in history are often explained in terms of the groups involved and their relative power. The outcomes of wars are often predicted in terms of alliances and the associated military strengths. History may look back with lofty terms like "truth", "honor", and "justice', but we have to take into account that the victors get to write the history. Truth may not be honored in the written account.

There were many elements of power when Christ faced crucifixion:

- There were the Jewish leaders and their forces.
- There were the formidable Roman forces.
- There were the unseen forces of evil.
- There were the people with their various views. They had little power.
- Peter tried to assert his power to protect his Savior, but the action was ill conceived.

There was one overwhelming force standing by. Christ mentioned it to Peter:

Matthew 26:52-53
52 "Put your sword back in its place," Jesus said to him, "for all who draw the sword will die by the sword.
53 Do you think I cannot call on my Father, and he will at once put at my disposal more than twelve legions of angels?

This is clearly a force beyond imagination, unseen by those who thought they were in power over the situation.

So which force prevailed? None mentioned so far! Christ died that day. The legions of angels remained uncalled. Christ remained faithful, even to death. There was yet one more force, and it did prevail:

It was love, God's love.

1 Corinthians 13:13
13 And now these three remain: faith, hope and love. But the greatest of these is love.

With faith in our Savior and hope in our hearts, we take these emblems of God's love, the greatest force on this earth.

Prayer for the Bread – The Emblem is Served

Prayer for the Wine–The Emblem is Served

THEME 13: SMYRNA
COMMUNION COMMENTS

It is time for Christians at this location to commune with our Lord. These emblems, the bread and the wine, represent respectively the body and blood of our Savior. It is a time of great respect and humility. We are directed to look deeply into our hearts and discern the body and blood of Christ on the cross. We are asked to remember the day He died for us.

Many of us enjoy comfortable financial circumstances. It could be easy to conclude that God's blessings in this regard result from a sort of entitlement based upon our upright lives. In that case, we might gather around the communion table with the pride of a people being honored. May such thoughts never be entertained.

The account of the message to the church at Smyrna in Revelation 2 will help us achieve a clearer understanding. The Lord acknowledged their tribulation, poverty and persecution. Furthermore, He told them that they would suffer yet more persecution. None of this came from any failure on their part. The Lord was pleased with them. He told them that, in the midst of earthly pain and poverty, they were rich. He told them one more wonderful thing that applies to us as well:

"Be faithful, even to the point of death, and I will give you the crown of life."

It is true that the Lord declares us to be a royal priesthood. We hold that title not as earned honor, but as His great gift of love to the undeserving. Let us partake with love and humility.

Prayer for the Bread – The Emblem is Served

Prayer for the Wine–The Emblem is Served

THEME 14: STRUGGLE
COMMUNION COMMENTS

We are all subject to the same tug-of-war described by Paul in Romans 7:14-7:25. Perhaps the central theme is summarized in this verse:

Romans 7:21
²¹ So I find this law at work: When I want to do good, evil is right there with me.

Paul describes the struggle further in:

1 Corinthians 9:24-27
²⁴ Do you not know that in a race all the runners run, but only one gets the prize? Run in such a way as to get the prize.
²⁵ Everyone who competes in the games goes into strict training. They do it to get a crown that will not last; but we do it to get a crown that will last forever.
²⁶ Therefore I do not run like a man running aimlessly; I do not fight like a man beating

the air.
²⁷ No, I beat my body and make it my slave
so that after I have preached to others, I
myself will not be disqualified for the prize.

Notice that Paul also suggests the ominous consequences of failure. What about Paul's "ever after" and ours? We can say of Paul that the struggle was always with him until execution. We have every reason to believe that he clung to Christ and left this world victorious. We cannot have the same confidence about Demas who may have lost his struggle:

2 Timothy 4:10
¹⁰ for Demas, because he loved this world,
has deserted me and has gone to Thessalon-
ica...

We who walk this earth are conflicted in our beings. The struggle goes on. Yet we cannot argue that we are simply victims of it. Paul asks and answers the salient question:

Romans 7:24-25
²⁴ What a wretched man I am! Who will res-
cue me from this body of death?
²⁵ Thanks be to God—through Jesus Christ
our Lord! So then, I myself in my mind am a
slave to God's law, but in the sinful nature a
slave to the law of sin.

John shared life with Christ. He furthers Paul's answer by describing the fellowship of joy that is ours to have:

1 John 1:5-9

⁵ This is the message we have heard from him and declare to you: God is light; in him there is no darkness at all.

⁶ If we claim to have fellowship with him yet walk in the darkness, we lie and do not live by the truth.

⁷ But if we walk in the light, as he is in the light, we have fellowship with one another, and the blood of Jesus, his Son, purifies us from all sin.

⁸ If we claim to be without sin, we deceive ourselves and the truth is not in us.

⁹ If we confess our sins, he is faithful and just and will forgive us our sins and purify us from all unrighteousness.

While we must carry this struggle while we are on the earth, Christ provides us the ability to walk in His light and, through His blood, ultimately stand before God innocent.

These emblems before us bring remembrance of the day when Christ paid the price for our ability to approach God with innocence. Let us partake with humility.

Prayer for the Bread – The Emblem is Served

Prayer for the Wine–The Emblem is Served

THEME 15: LOVE
COMMUNION COMMENTS

It is time for Christians at this location to commune with our Lord. These emblems before us, the bread and the fruit of the vine, represent respectively the body and blood of our Savior.

Many forces, both seen and unseen, were represented at the crucifixion. One force seldom mentioned in this regard was the most powerful of all. It was God's love for mankind. Paul discusses the power and beauty of love in I Corinthians 13. These comments will parallel some of the concepts there:

- It is possible for the comments and prayers to be fluent and appropriate,
- It is possible for the members to be respectful and focused on the crucifixion, and
- It is possible for the performance of the servers to be flawless.

But the actions of any member done without love are just empty show, a performance without substance except insult to the Lord.

Paul tells us that three things will remain with us after special gifts have passed: faith, hope and love.

- Our faith will confirm to us that our need to commune is real.
- Our hope will direct our focus to the time when our Savior will take us home,

And love, greatest of the three, will please God, honor our Savior, and bind us together in a holy temple of living stones.

Prayer for the Bread – The Emblem is Served

Prayer for the Wine–The Emblem is Served

THEME 16: HOLDING ON
COMMUNION COMMENTS

It is time for Christians at this location to commune with our Lord. These emblems, the bread and the wine, represent respectively the body and blood of our Savior. It is a time of great respect and humility. We are asked to remember the day He died for us.

The idea of communing implies something you do with others that is mutually beneficial. We can quickly prove from the scriptures:

- That God wants individual Christians to become members of a local church, and He wants them to come together with the church in regular assemblies.

- That God wants the local congregation to honor the practice of communion every Sunday.

The hope God has given us is precious, and He wants us to hold on with all our might and to encourage each other:

Hebrews 10:23-25
*23 Let us hold unswervingly to the hope we profess, for he who promised is faithful.
24 And let us consider how we may spur one*

another on toward love and good deeds.
25 Let us not give up meeting together, as
some are in the habit of doing, but let us
encourage one another—and all the more as
you see the Day approaching.

The love required to honor Christ in communion as described in I Corinthians 13 causes us to focus on the sacrifice of His body and blood. In doing so properly, our hearts are drawn closer to God, Christ, and each other.

Holding on requires considerable effort, but Christ has made His yoke easy. We must bring ourselves into subjection as Paul describes:

1 Corinthians 9:24-27
24 Do you not know that in a race all the run-
ners run, but only one gets the prize? Run in
such a way as to get the prize.
25 Everyone who competes in the games goes
into strict training. They do it to get a crown
that will not last; but we do it to get a crown
that will last forever.
26 Therefore I do not run like a man running
aimlessly; I do not fight like a man beating
the air.
27 No, I beat my body and make it my slave
so that after I have preached to others, I
myself will not be disqualified for the prize.

Communion can help focus our hearts on that objective.

Prayer for the Bread – The Emblem is Served

Prayer for the Wine–The Emblem is Served

THEME 17: THE MOST EXCELLENT WAY
COMMUNION COMMENTS

Christ had promised power to the apostles and it came unmistakably on the first Pentecost Day after His ascension. The Holy Spirit fell upon the apostles with a sound like a violent wind. The whole house where they were sitting saw what seemed to be tongues of fire come and rest upon each of them. They received many miraculous gifts. What a dramatic statement to the onlookers. They were "selected" for a great work, and no one there could deny.

One of the gifts they received was the ability to grant special gifts to others by the laying on of hands. Such gifts were needed to reach and convince potential new converts, and to teach the church as a whole. In a sense, the gifts were intended to give the fledgling new church a boost in the maturing process.

In Corinth, and perhaps other locations, those given gifts fell prey to using the gifts to compete with each other, thus missing the point. Paul pointed out the error of this behavior by teaching them "the most excellent way" in I Corinthians 13.

He told them the gifts were good, but they would pass, and in passing, leave three things: faith, hope, and love:

- Faith is the first thing that comes to us upon being taught the gospel message. It is the foundation for conversion.
- We are given the wonderful hope of eternal life.
- Love is the greatest of the three:
  - o God manifested His love for mankind when He allowed His Son to be crucified. He wants us to love Him in return.

  - o He wants us to love each other and not compete for attention. Love for one another is how members are identified.

  - o He wants us to show love and honor to Him and His Son by taking this memorial feast with our hearts and minds focused on Christ's sacrifice.

Let us cling in life and in this communion to:

"The Most Excellent Way"

Prayer for the Bread – The Emblem is Served

Prayer for the Wine–The Emblem is Served

THEME 18: VAST PRAISE
COMMUNION COMMENTS

The time has come for us to commune with our Lord. A time to remember His sacrifice for us and how it brought faith, hope, and love to brighten every day of our lives. These emblems before us, the bread and the fruit of the vine, represent respectively the body and the blood of our Savior.

Thoughts of the day and sometimes the inclination of our hearts may make it difficult to truly focus our minds on Christ's sacrifice. There is little question that Christ will be honored even if we fail to. John gives us a glimpse of the extent to which He is honored in a vision of Revelation:

> **Revelation 5:11-13**
> *[11] Then I looked and heard the voice of many angels, numbering thousands upon thousands, and ten thousand times ten thousand. They encircled the throne and the living creatures and the elders.*
> *[12] In a loud voice they sang: "Worthy is the Lamb, who was slain, to receive power and wealth and wisdom and strength and honor and glory and praise!"*
> *[13] Then I heard every creature in heaven and on earth and under the earth and on the sea,*

and all that is in them, singing: "To him who
sits on the throne and to the Lamb be praise
and honor and glory and power, for ever
and ever!"

It is possible to stand off to the side in our thoughts, not aligning with the celestial beings that are wiser and more powerful than us. On the other hand our thoughts can soar with them in tribute to the victorious Lamb. Now is such a time!

Prayer for the Bread – The Emblem is Served

Prayer for the Wine–The Emblem is Served

THEME 19: BACKDROP
COMMUNION COMMENTS

It is time for Christians at this location to commune with our Lord. These emblems, the bread and the wine, represent respectively the body and blood of our Savior. It is a time of great respect and humility. We are directed to look deeply into our hearts and discern the body and blood of Christ on the cross. We are asked to remember the day He died for us.

The advent of the church was the unfolding of a great dream of faith, love and hope. The paradox is that the dream is the solitary and greatest reality for mankind. The passing cultures surrounding the church, while perceived by most people to be the greatest reality, merely provide a moving backdrop for the church. The membership of the church is not recorded in any earthy document. The names of the redeemed are written in the Lamb's book of life in heaven.

The church is in this world but it is not of this world. The assurances we have from God, if we remain faithful, are certain. They are so certain that they are the most real of all things surrounding us. With these emblems, we acknowledge our love for the Savior.

The church, namely the redeemed, will remain "unshaken"

when Christ returns and this world ends. It is a kingdom on this earth, but its membership roll is in heaven.

Our Savior is with us in this communion. We are blessed with a place at this table.

Prayer for the Bread – The Emblem is Served

Prayer for the Wine–The Emblem is Served

THEME 20: THE CENTER
COMMUNION COMMENTS

Christ's death is positioned between two dispensations and between two Covenants. It is at the center of the reality in which we live, the most important event in all of history. The collective focus of Old Testament history points to Christ and His sacrifice:

- Many events and writings are shadows of the things to come in the advent of Christ on this earth,
- The line of kings descending from Judah pointed to the King to which the staff of power will belong forever, namely Christ.
- The tabernacle on the desert and temples to come were shadows of where the blood of Christ was taken in heaven.
- Many Old Testament prophesies look forward to the days when Christ would walk the earth and make His sacrificial journey to death.

On this side of the cross, we look back in this memorial communion to the day our Savior died for us. We join the chain of believers reaching back to the time of the cross:

- Our pattern of religious thought is the New Covenant as was theirs,
- The faith, hope and love that made their lives worthwhile now make our lives worthwhile,
- We also have a tabernacle in our walk on earth:
  - o It is built of living stones who are believers, and

  - o Its veil is open so that we can boldly approach God our Father in prayer.

All this is ours because Christ died for us. Our view in this communion looks back to His sacrifice for us, the center of our reality.

Prayer for the Bread – The Emblem is Served

Prayer for the Wine–The Emblem is Served

THEME 21:
PREFERENCE SURVEY
COMMUNION COMMENTS

It is not uncommon for companies, voters, churches, and other organizations of people to be presented with preference surveys. With this method it is possible to determine consensus, if there is one. Some organizations use preference surveys as a means to determine courses of action. Such surveys have a significant weakness in a church setting in that they are what they are–preferences.

For example, a preference survey about communion in the beginning days of the church in Corinth might have yielded interesting preferences in some:

- Preference for divisions between them, even during communion,
- Preference for a lavish feast and drunkenness more than focus on the Savior,
- Preference to humiliate the poor by not sharing, and
- Preference for groups and individuals to start whenever they chose, rather than commune together.

Paul had little praise for them. They were coming together for communion, but it may have done more harm than good.

Correcting the protocol of the communion might do little to correct the indicated problems in relationships between the factions.

Love was the missing element from their communions. They were showing little love for their Savior and little love for each other. Actually, they also cared little for Paul. The path from the attitudes in Corinth to those driving a vibrant, faithful congregation requires much growth.

Paul's messages remain for us, and we can honor Paul's instructions to achieve wonderful communions with our Savior and each other. Love can fill this building, and we can treat this communion and each other with honor and dignity.

Prayer for the Bread – The Emblem is Served

Prayer for the Wine–The Emblem is Served

THEME 22:
RIDING THE STORM
COMMUNION COMMENTS

Ezekiel was presented with an awesome vision of the majesty of God. He first saw a windstorm coming from the North. There was an immense cloud with flashing lightening and surrounded by brilliant light. In the midst were four Cherubim whose appearance was like burning coal, and fire moved back and forth among the creatures. It was bright and lightning flashed out of it. The creatures sped back and forth like lightening. Associated with each Cherub was a great wheel, sparkling as if it were made of precious stone. When the Cherubim moved, there would be a great rushing sound. There was a great throne above them, with an awesome individual on it with a figure like a man. There was brilliant light and radiance around Him and the appearance of a rainbow.

- There is much more detail than this paragraph presents, but it can be seen that the vision was awesome.
- It is a vision, but it is inconceivable that God would present Ezekiel with a vision of Himself that is inconsistent with His true majesty.

When presented with this vision of God, there is a question for us:

"Why would such a majestic being have a tender love for such as us?"

The question is hard to answer, but it should promote a deep gratitude within our hearts. Our awesome God of unbridled power watched His Son die on the cross because His heart is tender toward us. His Son also loved us so much that He left equality with God to die a bitter painful death on the cross for us.

These emblems before us represent His body and blood. Let us partake with a humility that befits the gift given us.

Prayer for the Bread – The Emblem is Served

Prayer for the Wine–The Emblem is Served

THEME 23:
STAND UP STRAIGHT
COMMUNION COMMENTS

Chapter 1 of the book of Luke records a time when God was preparing His people to receive a gift like no other, the Messiah. He sent John the Baptist to prepare the people to receive the gift. His responsibilities included the directive:

"to turn the hearts of the fathers to their children"

Parents sometimes show the inclinations of their hearts by giving gifts to their children, and we all know how excited they can become.

Loving parents deliver also simple messages to their children. Very often these messages seem to grow up, to mature, with the children. The simple messages become ever more important truths as the children become more able to understand. One such message most of us have heard:

"Stand Up Straight!"

To the very young child, there are only a few elements to it. None are complex. Parents may reinforce "Stand Up Straight!" with elements of meaning:

- People are watching!
- Act like you care!
- Don't embarrass me!

Later, the older child may be faced with speaking assignments in front of a group at church or school. What is the advice? **"Stand Up Straight!"** still has mileage to go. What does it mean now?

- Stand up straight if you want to impress anyone!
- If you slouch, no one will care what you say!
- Lean a little forward to let them know you are happy to be there.

Most young people will encounter a situation in life that severely tests them. Embarrassment, hurt feelings, lost love, exposure to accusation, and the like come along to knock on everyone's door eventually. What childhood admonition comes to the surface?

"Stand Up Straight!"

The expression is an old friend, but what does it mean now? How has it grown as the young person has aged?

- Pull yourself together!
- You still have great worth! God loves you, and so do we!
- Life will not end! You still have a job to do.
- Face this with truth and courage!

We Have a Father Whose Heart is Turned to Us

Here is a message that should grow within with each of us. We are to pull ourselves together. No matter what concerns us:

- God sees great worth in all of His family.
- Our lives will never end!
- Christ has the keys to the gates of death. He emerged and so will we.
- We face life with the truth of God's Covenant and the courage that comes from the meaning of this communion before us.
- In this way we **"Stand up straight!"**

Prayer for the Bread – The Emblem is Served

Prayer for the Wine–The Emblem is Served

THEME 24: CHRIST AND US
COMMUNION COMMENTS

Relationships we have with others are sometimes difficult to understand. This can bring misunderstandings, uncertainty, and stress. Even married couples may confess that they don't really understand each other. It is not uncommon for one to say to the other, "I don't really know who you are." In a relationship, we may think less of the other person than we should. It might also be true that our own self appraisal is too elevated.

We have a relationship with Jesus of Nazareth. Sometimes our behavior may reflect that we don't know well enough who He is. It may also be true that we don't exactly know who we are either. Hence, the relationship is unclear to us. Paul gives us insight in the first chapter of Colossians.

> **Colossians 1:15-23**
> *15 He is the image of the invisible God, the firstborn over all creation.*
> *16 For by him all things were created: things in heaven and on earth, visible and invisible, whether thrones or powers or rulers or authorities; all things were created by him and for him.*
> *17 He is before all things, and in him all*

things hold together.

[18] And he is the head of the body, the church; he is the beginning and the firstborn from among the dead, so that in everything he might have the supremacy.

[19] For God was pleased to have all his fullness dwell in him,

[20] and through him to reconcile to himself all things, whether things on earth or things in heaven, by making peace through his blood, shed on the cross.

[21] Once you were alienated from God and were enemies in your minds because of your evil behavior.

[22] But now he has reconciled you by Christ's physical body through death to present you holy in his sight, without blemish and free from accusation—

[23] if you continue in your faith, established and firm, not moved from the hope held out in the gospel. This is the gospel that you heard and that has been proclaimed to every creature under heaven, and of which I, Paul, have become a servant.

We are beings who sin and have no hope at all except through Christ. When we truly understand who He is and who we are, then we can achieve the humility to participate in this communion celebration in His honor.

Prayer for the Bread – The Emblem is Served.

Prayer for the Wine–The Emblem is Served

THEME 25: LOOKING BACK IN SORROW
COMMUNION COMMENTS

It is time for Christians at this location to commune with our Lord. These emblems, the bread and the wine, represent respectively the body and blood of our Savior. It is a time of great respect and humility. We are asked to remember the day He died for us.

Time runs only forward for humankind. Frequently, tragic occurrences could be averted if only we could turn time back just a little. John Greenleaf Whittier captured this thought in the poem <u>Maud Muller</u>:

> **For of all sad words of tongue or pen, the saddest are these, "It might have been!"**

These words can apply to many tragedies, to lost loves, to ill spoken words that cannot be pulled back. Most people have several occasions of this type to review. We often look back in sorrow. The news media is generously supplied with such accounts:

- The driver who failed to focus on his lane,
- The sea captain who failed to pay attention to the deep channel,
- The parent who failed to tend a child for only a

moment, and
- Words which should not have been spoken.

We can each add to the list. It is also easy to momentarily forget the price our Savior paid for us. When this happens, our spiritual armor leaves us vulnerable to the attacks of Satan. We can write events with the indelible ink of time that are shameful to remember.

God has given us this continual memoriam that we can share weekly. He requests that we remember His Son and the price He paid for us.

Prayer for the Bread – The Emblem is Served

Prayer for the Wine–The Emblem is Served

THEME 26: THE LAST TIME
COMMUNION COMMENTS

It is time for Christians at this location to commune with our Lord. These emblems, the bread and the wine, represent respectively the body and blood of our Savior. It is a time of great respect and humility. We are asked to remember the day He died for us.

The song we sang to prepare our minds was beautiful. Someday I will sing my last hymn on this earth. It probably won't be today, but it is likely that a Christian somewhere will do so.

Someday I will commune with Christ and my church family for the last time. Someday I will. If I could recognize that a communion before me was my last, what would my thoughts be?

- Panic? Perhaps.
- Sorrow? Perhaps.
- Joy? Perhaps.
- Regret of badly spent time. Likely.

It's easy to spend time badly. I can do so right now by forgetting:

- That Christ died for us,
- That the price of a future life for us was the cross for Jesus,

- That if I don't cherish this time of communion, I will lose the beauty of these precious moments.

Prayer for the Bread – The Emblem is Served

Prayer for the Wine–The Emblem is Served

THEME 27: HEAR, O ISRAEL
COMMUNION COMMENTS

God gave Moses many things to tell the people before entry into Canaan. Our lives are enhanced and productive if we can focus upon the things that are truly important. To do so, we must seek God's wisdom and revelation. Moses delivers God's instruction to Israel:

> **Deuteronomy 6:4-9**
> *⁴ Hear, O Israel: The Lord our God, the Lord is one.*
> *⁵ Love the Lord your God with all your heart and with all your soul and with all your strength.*
> *⁶ These commandments that I give you today are to be upon your hearts.*
> *⁷ Impress them on your children. Talk about them when you sit at home and when you walk along the road, when you lie down and when you get up.*
> *⁸ Tie them as symbols on your hands and bind them on your foreheads.*
> *⁹ Write them on the doorframes of your houses and on your gates.*

The communion we are observing this morning has the same thrust as these beautiful verses from Deuteronomy:

- We are celebrating God's great gift to mankind. He has shown His great love for us, and in return we show our love and respect for Him,
- Notice how precious the Old Covenant was to Israel. They were commanded to do things that reminded them of God's gift and especially to teach their children,
- We cannot think deep thoughts of the coming of the Messiah without remembering from Luke 1:17 that the "preparer", John the Baptist, had the responsibility:

"...to turn the hearts of the fathers to their children...", and

- Christ would deliver a New Covenant to Earth. His blood is the ransom for the faithful of the Old Covenant and for we who are blessed with the New Covenant.
- We observe this communion every week. When we observe it, there is one primary focus:

Jesus Christ Died For Us.

Prayer for the Bread – The Emblem is Served

Prayer for the Wine–The Emblem is Served

THEME 28:
IT WAS MEANT TO BE
COMMUNION COMMENTS

It is time for Christians at this location to commune with our Lord. These emblems, the bread and the wine, represent respectively the body and blood of our Savior. It is a time of great respect and humility. We are asked to remember the day He died for us.

Have you ever heard the expression, "It was meant to be."? It can have a variety of meanings, depending on context:

- It is sometimes used when something unexpectedly good has happened, so good it begs an explanation.
- Sometimes we use it as a lament to explain an unhappy outcome. It would not have happened unless "It was meant to be".
- Sometimes it is used to mitigate guilt when we want to indicate that the consequences of an action we took somehow involved broader forces.

In all of these cases, it is quite uncertain if the given event was actually "meant to be".

We can, however, say with certainty that Christ was meant to die on the cross for all mankind. It was meant to be. It was also meant to be that Christians would gather around communion tables like this one to honor their Savior in this solemn feast.

It was in God's mind when:

- He told Abraham that all mankind would be blessed through his seed.
- An aging Jacob prophesied that the line of Judah would bring forth a great King who would have an eternal kingdom.
- The great prophet Isaiah prophesied about Christ's life and sacrificial death.

It was truly meant that Christ would die for the faithful under both the Old Covenant and the New Covenant. It was meant for us to honor our Savior with this communion before us.

Prayer for the Bread – The Emblem is Served

Prayer for the Wine–The Emblem is Served

THEME 29: BE THERE
COMMUNION COMMENTS

It is time for Christians at this location to commune with our Lord. These emblems, the bread and the wine, represent respectively the body and blood of our Savior. It is a time of great respect and humility. We are asked to remember the day He died for us.

When the apostles and other inspired men went forth to teach the gospel, they converted large groups, small groups, and individuals. God never intended for individuals to intentionally be alone in their worship. We are reminded in Hebrews that we should assemble together:

Hebrews 10:24-25
[24] And let us consider how we may spur one another on toward love and good deeds. [25] Let us not give up meeting together, as some are in the habit of doing, but let us encourage one another—and all the more as you see the Day approaching.

We have come together today in compliance, and our Savior is with us. There are many reasons for meeting together; they include:

· The strength and encouragement in unity,

- The emotional needs served by being with kindred spirits, and
- The identity confirmed by communing together.

A somewhat puzzling construction of English is found in the maxim, "Wherever you are, be there." The idea expressed is that we need to keep our minds on where we are and what we are doing.

Our communion needs to be taken with the immediacy of being one in heart with our Savior and with each other.

Prayer for the Bread – The Emblem is Served

Prayer for the Wine–The Emblem is Served

THEME 30:
HILLS AND VALLEYS
COMMUNION COMMENTS

It is time for Christians at this location to commune with our Lord. These emblems, the bread and the wine, represent respectively the body and blood of our Savior. It is a time of great respect and humility. We are asked to remember the day He died for us.

Most of us are strong in the face of prosperity, health, and happiness. Most of us will occasionally face:

- Difficult situations,
- Life closing in on us, and
- Clusters of adverse factors.

For some of us, there seems to be no life to live except a sad one. How does one cope with the uncertainties life can present us? Happiness is difficult to sustain. To some it is a series of hills and valleys. To others, there may only be the continuation of a miserable life. We try to raise our kids so they can cope, but we sometimes wonder if we ourselves understand. God gives us some coping information and assurance of a happy future. Yet it is difficult to focus on these great blessings while our immediate circumstances bring us deep hurt.

One method of coping with a present sadness is to lift up our eyes to a future that is better, to focus on the distant view. Those who are God's children have already come to Mount Zion. Our names are written in the Lamb's Book of Life. When the end comes for created things, the church will remain "unshaken". This aging earth will pass, and our sorrows will pass with it. We gather about this table as God's Royal Priesthood to honor His Son. If we could see into heaven and read our names in the Book of Life, I am confident that our hearts would be prepared to partake of this communion.

Prayer for the Bread – The Emblem is Served

Prayer for the Wine–The Emblem is Served

THEME 31: FOCUS
COMMUNION COMMENTS

Great ambitions have resulted in many admirable accomplishments. We seldom respect people who have little ambition. There is one ambition that excels all others in importance; that is to live with one's creator for eternity. The hearts of the faithful yearn to be with God after life on earth is over. The price for God was high, the sacrifice of His Son. The price for us is that we remain faithful even to the point of death.

However, there are distractions impeding our path. There are so many ambitions that drive our hearts. Some can easily become all consuming pursuits. Some ambitions become so strong that all others are pushed out. Thoughts of God are simply displaced by a profusion of other attractions. Some of the possible pursuits are in and of themselves good and proper as long as we don't lose focus:

- o Our work,
- o Our business,
- o Money to raise a family,
- o Sports, entertainment, and
- o The list goes on …

These emblems before us represent the awful price paid for us to have the hope of eternity with God. They represent the central theme of the focus God wants us to have:

- The body and blood of Christ, His sacrifice,
- The love God has for us and the love we must return,
- The sacrifice for us,
- The remembrance and refocusing each week, and
- The remembrance that we are all fellow servants.

Prayer for the Bread – The Emblem is Served

Prayer for the Wine–The Emblem is Served

THEME 32: HEROIC DEEDS
COMMUNION COMMENTS

It is time for Christians at this location to commune with our Lord. These emblems, the bread and the wine, represent respectively the body and blood of our Savior. It is a time of great respect and humility. We are asked to remember the day He died for us.

There was war between Israel and the Philistines and David was in a stronghold when he made a wish:

> **2 Samuel 23:15**
> [15] *David longed for water and said, "Oh, that someone would get me a drink of water from the well near the gate of Bethlehem!"*

There were three of David's chief men with him. They were referred to as his "mighty men" and indeed they were. They took David's thought deeply to heart. The problem was that the Philistine line was between them and Bethlehem. In fact, the Philistine garrison was at Bethlehem. The three mighty men broke through the Philistine resistance and brought water from the well near the gate to David. David could not bring himself to drink it. It was too precious. Their sacrifice was too great. He poured it out as an offering to God:

> **2 Samuel 23:17**
> [17] *"Far be it from me, O Lord, to do this!" he said.*

"Is it not the blood of men who went at the risk of their lives?" And David would not drink it. Such were the exploits of the three mighty men.

How do we view the three mighty men?

· They were indeed mighty; they take their place as great Biblical heroes,
· Their respect for David was likely unequaled in his kingdom.
· They were not held back by fear.

Many of us today would like to do something heroic for our Lord. Not many of us have the capabilities of David's mighty men. While our hearts may be just as faithful, we may not have a similar opportunity.

Sometimes our view is not aligned with the Savior's view. He saw the widow's mite as contribution that was way beyond adequate. While we wait for an opportunity to make a heroic gesture, we may miss the plea of the Lord to do what He asked of Peter, "to feed His sheep". Acts of kindness to "His sheep" and the respect of a servant to his Lord may not bring fame, but is that not the message of our Lord who washed His apostle's feet? Is not the heart we present to Him during this communion of great importance? Do we not build a right heart with the simple deeds of love to those who walk the earth with us?

Prayer for the Bread – The Emblem is Served

Prayer for the Wine–The Emblem is Served

THEME 33:
PAYING FORWARD
COMMUNION COMMENTS

It is time for Christians at this location to commune with our Lord. These emblems, the bread and the wine, represent respectively the body and blood of our Savior. It is a time of great respect and humility. We are asked to remember the day He died for us.

"Paying forward" is an expression of our times. The idea, stated roughly, is that good deeds projected toward future needs of others eventually benefit everyone involved. It's even better if the deeds are anonymously done. This concept is soundly supported by the scriptures. Consider the often quoted admonition of Christ:

> **Matthew 6:19-21**
> [19] *"Do not store up for yourselves treasures on earth, where moth and rust destroy, and where thieves break in and steal.*
> [20] *But store up for yourselves treasures in heaven, where moth and rust do not destroy, and where thieves do not break in and steal.*
> [21] *For where your treasure is, there your heart will be also.*

Also, consider the wise observation in Ecclesiastes:

Ecclesiastes 11:1-2
¹ Cast your bread upon the waters, for after
many days you will find it again.
² Give portions to seven, yes to eight, for you
do not know what disaster may come upon
the land.

Stated in another way, "What we share forward will come back to us."

"Paying forward" does not always involve material goods. Sometimes it is a matter of kind words or honor paid. Such deeds create a right environment for the church. Members and visitors alike find a nurturing setting. As we participate in this communion, we show gratitude and honor to our God and our Savior. Our thoughts and hearts are on display as we show love for the love shown us. It would be better when we depart this life to have shown our love and gratitude in the communions we shared with each other and our Savior. Let us properly discern the body and the blood as we partake.

Prayer for the Bread – The Emblem is Served

Prayer for the Wine–The Emblem is Served

THEME 34:
WHISPERED HELP
COMMUNION COMMENTS

There was an aged couple in a congregation where I was once a member. Their hair was as white as snow. She was much shorter than he. They were ultra-faithful in attendance. He was on the list of men to lead prayers. It was custom there for most of the prayers to be lead from the pews rather than from the front. His prayers were quite predictable; in fact, he almost always said the same things. One time, the prayer came to a halt because he forgot where he was in the prayer and just fell silent. There he stood, silent and puzzled. I and others looked up to determine why the silence.

His little wife was standing on her tiptoes, whispering in his ear. He then continued the prayer. She had heard the prayer many times, and probably told him what he was about to say.

Some might consider that a problem needing correction. He could simply be taken off the list. After all, there is a need to put forth the best talent. Everything must be in order. So would go an efficient management view.

And Yet ...

Has something been missed in such a view. Are there no other considerations? Is there not something precious about a white haired couple walking into the sunset with God? Perhaps he was more forgetful, but would anyone contend that his prayers would not be heard because of repetition. What is God's disposition on such situations?

Leviticus 19:32
32 "'Rise in the presence of the aged, show respect for the elderly and revere your God. I am the Lord.

Proverbs 16:31
31 Gray hair is a crown of splendor; it is attained by a righteous life.

It is possible to achieve excellent form void of the substance God wants. In our communions, we open our arms of love to the entire body. We are of differing capabilities and resources, but we are all invited by our Lord. Our communions truly have substance when our embrace is for the body whole and our hearts are full of love for the Lord's sheep.

Prayer for the Bread – The Emblem is Served

Prayer for the Wine–The Emblem is Served

THEME 35:
THE BAPTISTRY BEHIND ME
COMMUNION COMMENTS

It is time for Christians at this location to commune with our Lord. These emblems, the bread and the wine, represent respectively the body and blood of our Savior. It is a time of great respect and humility. We are asked to remember the day He died for us.

Most communion messages are delivered while standing in front of or near to a baptistry. A proper baptism is the consummating event that brings one into Christ's church. Many have experienced baptism in rivers, creeks, cattle ponds, swimming pools, or even in such circumstances as deep fountains or bath tubs. Baptism is a monumental event at the beginning of a life as a Christian:

Colossians 2:9-15
⁹ For in Christ all the fullness of the Deity lives in bodily form,
¹⁰ and you have been given fullness in Christ, who is the head over every power and authority.
¹¹ In him you were also circumcised, in the

putting off of the sinful nature, not with a
circumcision done by the hands of men but
with the circumcision done by Christ,
[12] having been buried with him in baptism
and raised with him through your faith in
the power of God, who raised him from the
dead.
[13] When you were dead in your sins and in
the uncircumcision of your sinful nature,
God made you alive with Christ. He forgave
us all our sins,
[14] having canceled the written code, with its
regulations, that was against us and that
stood opposed to us; he took it away, nailing
it to the cross.
[15] And having disarmed the powers and
authorities, he made a public spectacle of
them, triumphing over them by the cross.

The price for salvation to be possible was the death of our
Savior on the cross. The victory came when He came forth
from the grave. This communion remembers Christ's sacrifice and reminds Christians weekly that we were redeemed
at great price. The thoughts of baptism remind us that there
are many who have not placed their lives with Christ. Christians carry a precious blessing that begs to be shared. It is
good to remember that our Savior has as many places at the
table as are needed for converts. His salvation is for all who
reach out and accept it. As His servants, our hearts should
yearn to tell the world about Him.

We gather about this table expressing the oneness that Christ
so wants of His church. We provide praise and honor to Him
in remembering His body and blood.

Prayer for the Bread – The Emblem is Served

Prayer for the Wine–The Emblem is Served

THEME 36: JOY COMPLETE
COMMUNION COMMENTS

It is time to remember the crucifixion of our Lord. These emblems before us, the bread and the wine, represent respectively the body and blood of Jesus. It is a time when we pay great respect.

The apostle John walked the earth with our Savior. He urged us to walk together in the light, along the path of truth:

1 John 1:1-4
¹ That which was from the beginning, which we have heard, which we have seen with our eyes, which we have looked at and our hands have touched—this we proclaim concerning the Word of life.
² The life appeared; we have seen it and testify to it, and we proclaim to you the eternal life, which was with the Father and has appeared to us.
³ We proclaim to you what we have seen and heard, so that you also may have fellowship with us. And our fellowship is with the Father and with his Son, Jesus Christ.
⁴ We write this to make our joy complete.

John can speak with authority about the nature of the Savior, for he was there with Him. Though we were not there, we have been told much about His nature. John appeals with us to have fellowship with Christ's apostles. Our fellowship is not just with each other. It is with God, Christ, the apostles, and with all Christians in all generations since Christ's time on the earth. When this is the case for us, then our joy is complete with all generations who have gathered about a communion table such as this.

Prayer for the Bread – The Emblem is Served

Prayer for the Wine–The Emblem is Served

THEME 37:
MEDLEY OF THOUGHTS
COMMUNION COMMENTS

It is time for Christians at this location to commune with our Lord. These emblems, the bread and the wine, represent respectively the body and blood of our Savior. It is a time of great respect and humility. We are asked to remember the day He died for us.

The Corinthians had severe problems with the conductance of the Lord's Supper. They had turned it into something that did more damage than good:

1 Corinthians 11:17
[17] In the following directives I have no praise for you, for your meetings do more harm than good.

- Communion had become a chaotic feast,
- The poor had less to eat than the well off,
- Some started before others, and
- Some got drunk.

It was a "communion" that amplified excesses and social separations. Unity of the church body and respect for the Savior were lost as a result. Paul pointed out these problems, and many congregations today have responded appropriately:

- · We begin and complete communion together,
- · The bread and wine are small emblematic portions, the same for everyone,
- · Love, respect, and unity are emphasized, and
- · Our Savior is the focus.

The form is correct and conducive to a respectful and proper communion. There is yet one element that cannot be seen as we observe the form. We can have all the form and yet not the substance. Our hearts and our thoughts need to be attuned to the Crucifixion of our Lord and what He did for us. Individually and together, our thoughts rise up to God in respect and gratitude. Let us all join hearts and minds as we commune together.

Prayer for the Bread – The Emblem is Served

Prayer for the Wine–The Emblem is Served

THEME 38: THE BEATITUDES
COMMUNION COMMENTS

It is time for Christians at this location to commune with our Lord. These emblems, the bread and the wine, represent respectively the body and blood of our Savior. It is a time of great respect and humility. We are asked to remember the day He died for us.

Matthew 5 records the message of Christ commonly called the *Sermon on the Mount.* Verses 3-12 are referred to as the *Beatitudes.* They reach into the heart so profoundly that most of us have deep feelings when we hear them. As a mother might place her hand on the forehead of a sick child, the Creator Savior placed His hand on the brow of a feverish, troubled humanity, speaking words of compassion and solace. The words carry a message of hope and much more. They were recorded for that generation and for all to come for all time.

Our Savior loves us ever so much. He is close to each one of us and He understands the human situation. He can look into our hearts and understand our frailties and our deepest fears. He is with us in this communion. Unlike the time when the *Sermon on the Mount* was delivered, we can look back on the death He died for all humanity. That is the focus of the communion we now take.

During communions, He also delivers a strong message. He provides us with a seat at His table, telling us that we are of His family. Just as the early Christians, we are provided a weekly reminder of His love and compassion. Just as He begins the beatitudes:

Blessed are we who are invited to this communion.

Prayer for the Bread – The Emblem is Served

Prayer for the Wine–The Emblem is Served

THEME 39: IN THE SHADOW OF THE CROSS
COMMUNION COMMENTS

It is time for Christians at this location to commune with our Lord. These emblems, the bread and the wine, represent respectively the body and blood of our Savior. It is a time of great respect and humility. We are asked to remember the day He died for us.

True success in an endeavor usually requires dedication. Some learn this truth early in life, some learn later, and some never learn. Many who become successful identify strongly with their work and they will express it freely, "I am a manager, sales person, carpenter, scientist, etc. Sometimes it is spoken with pride, sometimes too much pride.

The Bible certainly supports dedicated work:

Ecclesiastes 9:10
[10] Whatever your hand finds to do, do it with all your might, for in the grave, where you are going, there is neither working nor planning nor knowledge nor wisdom.

2 Thessalonians 3:10
[10] For even when we were with you, we gave you this rule: "If a man will not work, he shall not eat."

However, a life full of accomplishments can still be empty and misguided:

- If Christ does not come first,
- If personal pride drives our actions,
- If the cross is not in our hearts and our walk is not in its shadow, and
- If all of our accomplishments, great and small, have not been laid at the feet of Christ.

Christ spoke from the cross to His mother, Mary, as she looked up from the foot of the cross. No doubt, she could remember the aged Simeon's prophesy that her soul would be pierced. When our lives are lived in the shadow of the cross, we can always look up and, as Mary, behold our Savior's sacrifice for us.

We have this weekly communion

- To remind us of Christ's sacrifice for us
- To help us center our lives on the most important aspect
- To remind us that we should not leave the shadow of the cross.

Prayer for the Bread – The Emblem is Served

Prayer for the Wine–The Emblem is Served

THEME 40: FOUNDATIONS
COMMUNION COMMENTS

It is time for Christians at this location to commune with our Lord. These emblems, the bread and the wine, represent respectively the body and blood of our Savior. It is a time of great respect and humility. We are asked to remember the day He died for us.

The Bible has many references to foundations. The success or failure of an enterprise of mankind usually relies on the foundation that was laid beforehand. We all have a foundation from which we build our lives. It will involve the people we have known and the philosophies we have encountered. There are the "special" people who greatly influenced us. There are the works of literature and art that had impact. However, not all elements of one's foundation are worthy and solid. Some foundations divert people from the teachings of Christ. The result is instability.

Christ's words have stability and strength far stronger than rock. The New Covenant for which He paid with His blood provides a foundation lasting to eternity:

Matthew 7:24

²⁴ "Therefore everyone who hears these words of mine and puts them into practice is like a wise man who built his house on the rock.

David tells us who is blessed:

Psalms 1:2

² But his delight is in the law of the Lord, and on his law he meditates day and night.

We who gather around this communion table place our confidence in Christ and thus build our lives on the foundation of His truth.

Prayer for the Bread – The Emblem is Served

Prayer for the Wine–The Emblem is Served

THEME 41: A TIME TO BECOME A FOOL
COMMUNION COMMENTS

It is time for Christians at this location to commune with our Lord. These emblems, the bread and the wine, represent respectively the body and blood of our Savior. It is a time of great respect and humility. We are asked to remember the day He died for us.

There is a time when it is good to become a fool. The scriptures tell us when the time comes and the purpose of becoming a fool:

1 Corinthians 3:18
[18] Do not deceive yourselves. If any one of you thinks he is wise by the standards of this age, he should become a "fool" so that he may become wise.

Becoming a fool is likely not pleasant to an individual with an overly elevated appraisal of self worth. How might such a demotion come about?

- God has reduced the prideful to fools for their own benefit. Consider Nebuchadnezzar. God made him

insane so that he lived seven years as a beast in the
field. When his sanity returned, he honored and
glorified God.

· Sometimes arrogant behavior brings one the recog-
nition of being a fool:

Proverbs 11:2
*² When pride comes, then comes disgrace,
but with humility comes wisdom.*

· The individual may become self aware and make
the choice as an act of submission to Paul's admonition in I Corinthians 3:18.

This table is not for the arrogant. We are invited by an awesome God who is not impressed by the flaunted wisdom of
men. Our clothing is appropriate for a royal priesthood. We
are clothed in Christ. The places at the table are reserved for
the humble and the grateful.

Prayer for the Bread – The Emblem is Served

Prayer for the Wine–The Emblem is Served

THEME 42: KEEPING WINDOWS CLEAN
COMMUNION COMMENTS

Most of our homes have windows. Without them we feel constrained, cut off from the world outside. We also use the word "windows" in a more abstract way. Acquisition of knowledge opens "windows" of vision to see new paths and opportunities. One maxim seems to be true for all windows:

Windows Must Be Kept Clean To Be Useful

Baptism is a window into a different world. The people who heard Peter on the Day of Pentecost were told a simple truth that had everything to do with their salvation. They were deeply moved and responded immediately. There was no complex mysticism, no complicated instructions. Based upon their demonstrated faith that Jesus Christ is the Son of God and their obvious repentance, they were dipped in water as a symbolic burial with Christ. That window is clean. The view is accurate.

The New Covenant is a window into a new walk of life provided by a loving God because mankind could not meet the conditions of the Old Covenant. We are commanded to hear God as He speaks to us through the New Covenant:

Hebrews 12:25

[25] See to it that you do not refuse him who speaks. If they did not escape when they refused him who warned them on earth, how much less will we, if we turn away from him who warns us from heaven?

God's instructions to us may be profound, but the New Covenant is the window. That's clear. Hence, we must experience a proper baptism and live our lives in accordance with the New Covenant. These two windows are clean. The views are clear.

A Window of Remembrance

This communion today looks back through a window of remembrance to the day Christ died for us. The total meaning to Christians is vast. Vast love was shown by God the Father and His Son, Jesus Christ. The actions involved are straightforward. These two emblems, the bread and the fruit of the vine are just that, bread without yeast and the juice of grapes. They are symbolic of the body and blood of Jesus. Early Christians took them with prayer in the same way Christ indicated in His last Passover with His apostles. All this conforms to the New Covenant. This window is also clean.

As we partake, Father and Son have a window into our hearts. It is clean and the view is unimpeded. We must be mindful of the body and blood of Christ sacrificed for us.

Prayer for the Bread – The Emblem is Served

Prayer for the Wine–The Emblem is Served

THEME 43: DON'T FORGET WHO YOU ARE
COMMUNION COMMENTS

It is time for Christians at this location to commune with our Lord. These emblems, the bread and the wine, represent respectively the body and blood of our Savior. It is a time of great respect and humility. We are asked to remember the day He died for us.

How often has a parent said to an offspring going out for the evening, "Don't forget who you are."? The question implies at least the following instructions:

- Don't do anything below your dignity, and
- Don't bring shame on the family.

We have a noble identity. Just like a family name, it was given to us. Unlike a family name, it was assigned to us by a loving God. We are children of God. Even God's own Son is not ashamed to call us brothers:

Hebrews 2:11

[11] Both the one who makes men holy and those who are made holy are of the same family. So Jesus is not ashamed to call them brothers.

This communion is a time to remember Christ and His sacrifice for us. Our thoughts need to be focused. As a parent instructs an offspring, we can consider in our hearts this instruction:

- Our thoughts should be aligned with the dignity of these moments, and
- The manner in which we partake should not bring shame upon ourselves or this church family.

Let us honor God and our Savior with this sacred communion.

Prayer for the Bread – The Emblem is Served

Prayer for the Wine–The Emblem is Served

THEME 44:
THE FORTRESS AROUND US
COMMUNION COMMENTS

It is time for Christians at this location to commune with our Lord. These emblems, the bread and the wine, represent respectively the body and blood of our Savior. It is a time of great respect and humility. We are asked to remember the day He died for us.

God provides protection for the faithful. The thought of a fortress appeals to us when we feel surrounded by adverse forces. The Bible provides many instances of such protection. Sometimes the reality of it is straightforward and clearly seen and conventional such as the wall about Jerusalem. Sometimes the protection is just as real but unseen as the fiery chariots that protected Elisha in II Kings 6:15-17. In all cases, it is not the apparent forces, but rather the hand of God that provides the protection. Also, the promise is not that harm or death will not come our way, for they may. The promise is that no force on this earth or elsewhere can take us away from God if we remain faithful, Romans 8:37-39.

David relates in the beautiful Psalms 23 that God has prepared for him a table in the midst of his enemies. The person who can enjoy a meal while surrounded by enemies truly believes in the protection of God. Today we are surrounded by many enemies:

· We worry that our resources may be taken from us, but Hebrews 13:5 provides us this assurance:

Hebrews 13:5

*⁵ Keep your lives free from the love of money
and be content with what you have, because
God has said, "Never will I leave you; never
will I forsake you."*

There are many who might harm us for their own advantage, but Hebrews 13:6 says that we have the most powerful Helper of all:

Hebrews 13:6

*⁶ So we say with confidence, "The Lord is my
helper; I will not be afraid. What can man
do to me?"*

We fear the most frightening enemies, the unseen legions of spiritual enemies. They are inhuman forces, not flesh and blood. Our fortress of protection in this case is the spiritual armor described in Ephesians 6:10-18. God tells us in verse 13 that we will be able to stand:

Ephesians 6:13

*¹³ Therefore put on the full armor of God,
so that when the day of evil comes, you may
be able to stand your ground, and after you
have done everything, to stand.*

A table lies before us in the midst of our enemies. Let us show honor to Christ who gave us the victory through His blood.

Prayer for the Bread – The Emblem is Served

Prayer for the Wine–The Emblem is Served

THEME 45:
VISUALIZING CHRIST
COMMUNION COMMENTS

Artists have long attempted to produce paintings that capture the appearance and nature of Christ. It is likely that none walked with the Savior and knew Him personally. Most of us have some image of Him in our minds. We may ask ourselves questions:

- Was He tall, short, or of medium height?
- Was He dark or light skinned?
- What color were His eyes?

Would we recognize Him from the images we have built? A prophesy in Isaiah implies that many of the paintings may be incorrect:

Isaiah 53:2
2 He grew up before him like a tender shoot,
and like a root out of dry ground. He had no
beauty or majesty to attract us to him, nothing
in his appearance that we should desire him.

His appearance alone may not have greatly impressed people, but when He chose to, He could electrify an audience.

When the Jewish leaders sent the temple guards to arrest Him, they came back empty handed:

John 7:45-46
⁴⁵ Finally the temple guards went back to the chief priests and Pharisees, who asked them, "Why didn't you bring him in?"
⁴⁶ "No one ever spoke the way this man does," the guards declared.

His words in the Scriptures are profoundly true and lead to life eternal. How do we see Him in our minds today?

- Someone in first century Bible land clothing?
- Weeping alone at Gethsemane?
- Battered and torn on the cross?
- The Living One who emerged from death with the keys of death and Hades? The keys we desperately need?
- In Revelation, the Slaughtered Lamb on the throne seat of God?
- In Revelation, the awesome King who stood among the seven golden lamp stands holding the seven stars in His hand?

Now is the time for the mind's eye to pay honor and tribute to this Savior as we partake of these emblems representing His body and blood.

Prayer for the Bread – The Emblem is Served

Prayer for the Wine–The Emblem is Served

THEME 46: THE BEAUTY OF SIMPLE THINGS
COMMUNION COMMENTS

Our Savior presented us with many profound concepts in parables using simple things of everyday life. There are three simple things which are both common to human life and to this communion table before us. These are:

- Water,
- Fields of grain, and
- Vineyards

Christ elevated these common things to have profound meanings to His faithful. They appear throughout the scriptures intermingled with great truths. They are closely associated with living on this earth. If you were asked to find great concentrations of people in the Biblical times, these three simple elements of life would be involved. People located where there were fields of grain, vineyards, and drinkable water, often along rivers.

Psalms 1 describes an upright man whose delight is in God's law. He is likened to a tree planted by rivers of water. Christ told the Samaritan woman at the well that He could give her water so that she would never thirst again. Water is vital to human life. It is likened to the thirst that those about the communion table must have to honor God's New Covenant.

The bread and the fruit of the vine on this communion table come from fields of grain and vineyards. These crops will support human life, but Christ elevated these emblems to represent His body and blood. He sacrificed Himself so that we might have eternal life.

Christ represents Himself as the bread of life, the food we need to have spiritual life. It represents His body. There is a profound linkage with the body of the sacrificed Passover lamb. The shed blood, represented by the fruit of the vine, is referred to as the blood of the New Covenant. It paid for the New Covenant, the Law we are to love.

A further illustration in simple instructions for life eternal:

- A proper baptism, and then
- Remain faithful to God's New Covenant until death.

Prayer for the Bread – The Emblem is Served

Prayer for the Wine–The Emblem is Served

THEME 47: THE FULLNESS OF TIME
COMMUNION COMMENTS

It is time for Christians at this location to commune with our Lord. These emblems, the bread and the wine, represent respectively the body and blood of our Savior. It is a time of great respect and humility. We are asked to remember the day He died for us.

The biblical unfolding of history from the time of Adam's fall is an account of man's relationship with God. The age of the patriarchs preceded the Old Covenant and the nationhood of Israel. A future view was building all this time. Prophets looked forward to it, and great men of old yearned for it. The prophesies were not fully definitive, so the view of it was clouded, at least for some.

In God's Good Time, Christ Came to Earth

Some explain in retrospect all the reasons Christ came to earth when He did. Christ accused the leaders of the day in Matthew 16:1-4 of not recognizing the signs and His deity even when He was standing among them. The "fullness of time" and the decisions required to bring it into being was God's job. Our job is to be filled with awe and appreciation. Christ's death on the cross served many purposes:

- He obeyed His Father,
- He reconciled mankind to God,
- He brought the adoption of Gentiles into the Commonwealth of Israel,
- He paid for the New Covenant with His Blood.

In God's Good Time, Christ Will Return

Christ will return again to claim His own. Affairs of this earth will end:

2 Peter 3:8-13

[8] But do not forget this one thing, dear friends: With the Lord a day is like a thousand years, and a thousand years are like a day.

[9] The Lord is not slow in keeping his promise, as some understand slowness. He is patient with you, not wanting anyone to perish, but everyone to come to repentance.

[10] But the day of the Lord will come like a thief. The heavens will disappear with a roar; the elements will be destroyed by fire, and the earth and everything in it will be laid bare.

[11] Since everything will be destroyed in this way, what kind of people ought you to be? You ought to live holy and godly lives

[12] as you look forward to the day of God and speed its coming. That day will bring about the destruction of the heavens by fire, and the elements will melt in the heat.

[13] But in keeping with his promise we are looking forward to a new heaven and a new earth, the home of righteousness.

115

This anticipated event is an almost exclusive focus of many religious people. Predictions of its eminence have occurred many times over the centuries and are prevalent in today's world. We are commanded to study our Bibles, and the scriptures involving end times are part of it. We are provided some information about the decadence that will afflict the world immediately before the end, so prediction can be attempted. However, we are also told that the end will come as a thief in the night; that is, the event will be a surprise to whatever age experiences it.

Dealing With End Times by Paying Attention to the Present

Peter's discussion of the end times in II Peter 3 ends with an admonition for our reaction to the end times:

2 Peter 3:14-18
14 So then, dear friends, since you are looking forward to this, make every effort to be found spotless, blameless and at peace with him.
15 Bear in mind that our Lord's patience means salvation, just as our dear brother Paul also wrote you with the wisdom that God gave him.
16 He writes the same way in all his letters, speaking in them of these matters. His letters contain some things that are hard to understand, which ignorant and unstable people distort, as they do the other Scriptures, to their own destruction.
17 Therefore, dear friends, since you already know this, be on your guard so that you may not be carried away by the error of lawless men and fall from your secure position.

18 But grow in the grace and knowledge of our Lord and Savior Jesus Christ. To him be glory both now and forever! Amen.

The solution for a Christian is to take care of the present:

- · We are to live pure upright lives,
- · We are to avoid being carried away by people who twist the scriptures for their own purposes, and
- · We are to steadfastly grow in the grace and knowledge of our Savior.

We are the people of the New Covenant, and we have a job to do. We need to spread the message of Christ. The hope we have and the hope we spread was paid for by the blood of Christ. This communion table before us is a continual memorial to recognize Christ's sacrifice. It is also a reminder of who we are and what God wants of us.

We share this memorial with all generations past and future from the time Christ came and died for us until He comes again to claim His own.

Prayer for the Bread – The Emblem is Served

Prayer for the Wine–The Emblem is Served

THEME 48:
HUNG IT ON NOTHING
COMMUNION COMMENTS

It is time for Christians at this location to commune with our Lord. These emblems, the bread and the wine, represent respectively the body and blood of our Savior. It is a time of great respect and humility. We are asked to remember the day He died for us.

The Lord described Job to Satan as follows:

- No man like him,
- Blameless,
- Upright,
- Fears God, and
- Shuns evil.

Job was close to God and he knew many things. One of the things he knew has a lot to do with the communion we take today. What could Job have known about God's mysteries, and why should we accept any comments of his related to Christ? First, let us establish Job's credentials with respect to unexpected knowledge. Job made a remarkable statement about the earth:

Job 26:7

*⁷ He spreads out the northern [skies] over
empty space; he suspends the earth over
nothing.*

We all know that! We know about orbits, solar systems, gravity, and things like that. We can look at pictures from rockets and see pictures of the earth just hanging there ... suspended on nothing. Question is, "How did Job know that, centuries upon centuries before it would be prevalent in the scientific world?" We can stand upon the shoulders of such men as Galileo, Copernicus, Kepler, Newton, and others in the very recent past compared to Job's era. Job had a very special insight. God Himself declared there was no man like him!

What about Christ? Did Job know anything about Christ? Did Job see through his misery to any other unknown mysteries? Consider these verses:

Job 16:19-21

*¹⁹ Even now my witness is in heaven; my
advocate is on high.
²⁰ My intercessor is my friend as my eyes
pour out tears to God;
²¹ on behalf of a man he pleads with God as
a man pleads for his friend.*

Job 19:25-27

*²⁵ I know that my Redeemer lives, and that in
the end he will stand upon the earth.
²⁶ And after my skin has been destroyed, yet*

in my flesh I will see God;
²⁷ I myself will see him with my own eyes—I,
and not another. How my heart yearns with-
in me!

Job knew he had someone to plead for him with God. Job knew that long after his death, his Redeemer would stand on the earth. Job knew that someday he would see God.

Our Redeemer did come to earth, and He sealed His plea for Job and for us with His own blood on the cross. This memorial feast remembers Christ's great sacrifice.

Prayer for the Bread – The Emblem is Served

Prayer for the Wine–The Emblem is Served

THEME 49:
WALKING WITH GOD
COMMUNION COMMENTS

It is time for Christians at this location to commune with our Lord. These emblems, the bread and the wine, represent respectively the body and blood of our Savior. It is a time of great respect and humility. We are asked to remember the day He died for us.

The expression "Walk with God" is used frequently. Sometimes it is an admonition; sometimes it is a wish for future blessings. The expression rolls off the tongue easily, and it usually comes from people who love you.

The idea of actually walking with God or Christ is almost too awesome to contemplate. Genesis speaks of God walking in the garden in the cool of the evening. There is implication that Adam and Eve sometimes walked with Him, because they hid from Him after eating the forbidden fruit. We have a strong indication of just how far they fell. Both Abraham and Moses spoke to God directly.

John tells us how it was for the apostles to be with Jesus, to see, touch, and hear Him as they experienced life together:

1 John 1:1-4
¹ That which was from the beginning, which we have heard, which we have seen with our eyes, which we have looked at and our

hands have touched—this we proclaim con-
cerning the Word of life.
² The life appeared; we have seen it and
testify to it, and we proclaim to you the eter-
nal life, which was with the Father and has
appeared to us.
³ We proclaim to you what we have seen and
heard, so that you also may have fellowship
with us. And our fellowship is with the Fa-
ther and with his Son, Jesus Christ.
⁴ We write this to make our joy complete.

It remains difficult to imagine actually walking on this earth with Christ.

During this communion, we are asked to walk with Christ in our minds as we take these emblems of His body and blood. We can be with Him in Gethsemane and Golgotha. We can hear in our minds the words of Matthew where Christ cries out to His Father:

Matthew 27:46
⁴⁶ About the ninth hour Jesus cried out in
a loud voice, "Eloi, Eloi, lama sabach-
thani?"—which means, "My God, my God,
why have you forsaken me?"

We can contemplate that the Father didn't stop the crucifixion because He loves us. We can contemplate that the Son didn't request twelve legions of angels because He loves us.

Prayer for the Bread – The Emblem is Served

Prayer for the Wine–The Emblem is Served

THEME 50:
WHAT ABOUT CALEB?
COMMUNION COMMENTS

It is time for Christians at this location to commune with our Lord. These emblems, the bread and the wine, represent respectively the body and blood of our Savior. It is a time of great respect and humility. We are asked to remember the day He died for us.

The scriptures have many accounts of meritorious people. Sometimes their names appear again and again because remembrance inspires many generations. God does not provide us with detailed information of how the choice is made to include or not include people of merit in subsequent Holy Spirit inspired writings. Joshua is often mentioned, and there is little question, Old Testament or New, that he was a great man of faith. However, his name remains so tied to the name Caleb that it is difficult to separate the two when talking about Old Testament heroes. As spies, they saw Canaan as a wonderful land awaiting conquest by Israel. They made their spy journey with eyes of faith. The other spies made the trip with eyes of fear. Thus we have two great warriors for God, Joshua and Caleb. Joshua is much heralded, and Caleb not so much.

Joshua and Caleb were the only two of their generation to go into the Promised Land. The curse of God was upon the adults who repeatedly displayed lack of faith. Their bones were left in the desert after 40 years of wandering.

There is a parallel with this communion. Few, if any, of us will be remembered strongly through the ages. The important issue is that our thoughts come from hearts of faith and dedication. We should have full confidence to enter God's rest by the power of Christ's sacrifice. Caleb was not left out, and he probably was not competing for equal credit. He did his job, and he presented a right heart to God when he spied out Canaan. In like manner, let us present right hearts in this communion.

Prayer for the Bread – The Emblem is Served

Prayer for the Wine–The Emblem is Served

THEME 51: NEEDING
COMMUNION COMMENTS

Paul described some aspects of God to the Greek Areopagus as follows:

Acts 17:25-27

25 And he is not served by human hands, as if he needed anything, because he himself gives all men life and breath and everything else. 26 From one man he made every nation of men, that they should inhabit the whole earth; and he determined the times set for them and the exact places where they should live. 27 God did this so that men would seek him and perhaps reach out for him and find him, though he is not far from each one of us.

Unlike idols men have chosen for themselves, God doesn't need human hands to feed, house, or carry Him about. He has no needs of that type.

The Verses tell us two things that God chose for us:

1. We are living in a chosen period of time, and

2. We are in this exact place.

It is not a far reach that our presence together this morning is not an accident of probability.

What was God's reason? From Verse 27, "so that men would seek Him".

God certainly has wants. Among them, He wants His sheep to be fed, as Christ instructed Peter, and He wants mankind to reach out to Him. This brings a question, "Will we accuse God of having wants He does not need?" That is a common failure to humankind, but not to God!

Do we have needs? Indeed we do, and one is a desperate need to reach out to our God. With this communion before us, we can reach out to Him:

- Sincerely,
- Together, with unified hearts,
- Accurately, as described in the New Covenant,
- With honor to our Lord and Savior,
- Discerning His body and blood,
- With acknowledgment that He died for us, and
- With a steadfast resolve to stand firmly on Mount Zion with the redeemed of the ages.

Prayer for the Bread – The Emblem is Served

Prayer for the Wine–The Emblem is Served

THEME 52: BUILDING A TEMPLE
COMMUNION COMMENTS

Power came dramatically to the apostles on Pentecost Day, and there were many added to Lord's church following their baptisms. The message of Christ began to spread. It was preached to large groups, small groups, and to individuals. Converts began to be grouped into congregations, and the apostles began to deliver the truths and commandments given them by the Holy Spirit on Pentecost. Some additional men were given special gifts by the laying on of the apostle's hands. The writings of the apostles and these inspired men would ultimately be gathered together as the New Testament. Embodied within it is God's New Covenant. How important were these teachings? Faithfulness was and is today mandatory. Revelation 2:10 includes the following admonition to a congregation at Smyrna:

> ... *"Be faithful, even to the point of death,*
> *and I will give you the crown of life."*

Salvation for the early convert and for us today requires the fidelity to God's teachings until death. Paul gave this admonition in I Corinthians 4:6:

> ... *"Do not go beyond what is written."*

*Then you will not take pride in one man over
against another.*

The faithful walk is directed by definitive instructions which
are not to be embellished nor appended by non-apostolic
sources. Early Christians came together by way of command
and not by preference:

Hebrews 10:25
*[25] Let us not give up meeting together, as
some are in the habit of doing, but let us
encourage one another—and all the more as
you see the Day approaching.*

The entire New Covenant has been complete since the early years of the church. It directs the mission and activities of the congregations. The communion is a part of the New Covenant. Its significance embodies the spirit of our walk with Christ:

- It honors the sacrifice of our Savior,
- It acknowledges the oneness, the unity of the church,
- It acknowledges the love of God, and
- It is intended to be practiced until Christ returns.

We are to discern the body and blood of our Savior as we partake. Thoughts of the body should include thoughts of the church because it is referred as the body of Christ. Thoughts of the blood should remember that it was the purchase price for the New Covenant.

Every Christian has the challenge of becoming a living stone built together with the other members as a holy temple where

God dwells, namely the church of Jesus Christ.

Prayer for the Bread – The Emblem is Served

Prayer for the Wine–The Emblem is Served

CONCLUDING REMARKS

The theme of this book is the overwhelming fact personal to each Christian:

Christ died for me!

So began the concluding remarks of my previous book, *Glimpses of Communion"*. Some statements cannot be declared too many times! This second book of communion themes has been a rewarding journey for the author. Thoughts of the sacrifice by our Savior and the love God displayed for mankind bring both humility and gratitude.

The communions we have taken are time markers that line up in the respective corridors of our lives. Those of us with age have taken the emblems at times when life circumstances were joyful, sorrowful, chaotic, peaceful, painful, and the various emotional circumstances that befall mankind. The message of each communion is the same. It tells us that God's love is well proven by the sacrifice of His Son. We are assured that our continuance of faith until death will indeed bring us a crown. It is a beacon to bring us home.

May all your future communions with our Lord be meaningful and may you help your brothers and sisters come to a deeper understanding and appreciation for the greatest act of benevolence in history. God so loved the world that He gave

His one and only Son.

God Bless You All

Grady W. Troute

APPENDIX
PRESIDING OVER COMMUNION

These guidelines were copied directly from my first book devoted to communion, *Glimpses of Communion*. They are repeated here for your convenience.

Guidelines are the prerogatives of the leadership of the given congregation. The formulation of guidelines is needed if several different men are to be used as communion speakers. The objectives are straightforward.

- The congregation needs to be moved to the proper mindset to partake,
- Visitors need to know what is happening. This may take the form of knowledge accumulated during several communions. There is no imperative to deliver a comprehensive explanation each time, and
- Christ and scripture must be honored.

I believe the following guidelines will help the quality of the communion speaker's effectiveness.

1. The issue of dress will eventually come up. The speaker's attire should not defeat the intended objectives.

2. The speaker, as all who have a role in the service, should arrive as early as the leadership designates. This is necessary for the coordinator(s) to accomplish their job.

3. There should be a time limit for the comments. The comments should not be considered a "sermonette".

4. The following guidelines apply to the comments themselves:

    - The occasion and mood are sober. Humor in the comments is improper.
    - Christ is the center of the comments. Those redeemed commune with their Savior. Nothing should detract from this theme.
    - There is no parallel in all of human history to the event of God's Son dying for humanity. Comparisons to deeds of others, living or dead, however meritorious, detract from Christ in most cases.
    - Personal stories that bring focus on the speaker, the speaker's family, the speaker's job, the speaker's favorite theme, etc. are off point and must be avoided.
    - There are many good causes. None are good enough to detract from Christ during the communion comments.
    - Our visitors need to know why we take communion. Our members need to prepare their minds to partake properly. There should never be a question in a listener's mind as to the focus of the comments.

These guidelines may seem too constraining to some. However, there is one overpowering reality to be served:

THE FOCUS IS CHRIST!

Grady W. Troute

CPSIA information can be obtained at www.ICGtesting.com
Printed in the USA
LVOW10s0215200913

353281LV00001B/1/P